Exploring
Ruth

Finding hope. Restoring Heritage.

One family's courageous journey from tragedy to amazing success.

DAVID HENRY

Bring the books, especially the Parchments

Parchments, LLC
PO Box 277
Shawnee OK 74802
www.parchments.net
Phone:

© 2014. David Henry. All rights reserved.

No part of this work may be reproduced, stored in a retrieval system,
or transmitted in any form or by any means, electronic or mechanical,
including photocopying and recording, without the written permission of the author.

First printed by David Henry 2012.

ISBN: 978-0-9960716-0-4 (sc)

Printed in the United States of America.

Ruth Bible Study Guide

Content

Unit 1	Ruth 1	**Making Good Decisions in Bad Times**			
_____	Week 1	Lesson 1	OBSERVATION:	Finding the Facts
_____	Week 2	Lesson 2	INTERPRETATION:	Drawing Good Conclusions
_____	Week 3	Lesson 3	APPLICATION:	Applying Biblical Principles
Unit 2	Ruth 2	**Following the Hand of Providence**		
_____	Week 4	Lesson 1	OBSERVATION:	Finding the Facts
_____	Week 5	Lesson 2	INTERPRETATION:	Drawing Good Conclusions
_____	Week 6	Lesson 3	APPLICATION:	Applying Biblical Principles
Unit 3	Ruth 3	**Pursuing the Life of a Virtuous Woman**		
_____	Week 7	Lesson 1	OBSERVATION:	Finding the Facts
_____	Week 8	Lesson 2	INTERPRETATION:	Drawing Good Conclusions
_____	Week 9	Lesson 3	APPLICATION:	Applying Biblical Principles
Unit 4	Ruth 4	**Accepting God's Blessings**		
_____	Week 10	Lesson 4.1	OBSERVATION:	Finding the Facts
_____	Week 11	Lesson 4.2	INTERPRETATION:	Drawing Good Conclusions
_____	Week 12	Lesson 4.3	APPLICATION:	Applying Biblical Principles
_____	Week 13		REVIEW & REFLECTION	

Making Big Decisions

Her name was Agnes Gonxha Bojaxhiu. She was born on August 26, 1910. Little did they know she would become an inspiration to leaders of nations and millions around the world. The turning point in Agnes' life took place around age 18 when she made the decision to commit herself to a religious life and become a missionary to Ireland. When she left home it was the last time she saw her mother and sister.

From the obscurity of her birth in Skopje, Macedonia. An ordinary woman rose to global prominence because of her devotion to the commitments she made.

She founded the *Missionaries of Charity* and led its work from 1950 until a few months before her death on September 5, 1997 at age 87. The *Missionaries of Charity* provides service to the poorest people around the world. In 2012 this organization consisted of over 4,500 sisters and operates in as many as 133 countries. These sisters take the vows of chastity, poverty, obedience, and give "Wholehearted and Free service to the poorest of the poor."

In 1979, Agnes was the recipient of the coveted Nobel Peace Prize. She refused the ceremonial banquet and asked that the $192,000 funds be given to the poor in India. Other honors were bestowed on her by countries such as the Philippines, Australia, the United Kingdom, the United States, and Albania.

Agnes Bojaxhiu died on September 5, 1997 at the age of 87. She was granted a state funeral and laid for viewing an entire week prior to the burial. Her death was mourned by both religious and secular communities.

In 2010, governments organized centennial celebrations in her honor. Germany issued a postage stamp commemorating her legacy. An airport is named in her honor. Her legacy is the subject of a documentary film in 1969 and the book *Something Beautiful for God* published in 1972.

If you see a picture of her face you would recognize her instantly. You and I know this ordinary woman as *Mother Teresa* of Calcutta, India. She made a great influence on Roman Catholicism around the world and is perhaps more recognizable than the Pope.

The book of Ruth tell the story of another ordinary young lady from Moab who made a big decision that transformed her life and inspires generations. Ruth was an ordinary lady with extraordinary strength of character. That strength is reflected in the personal, social, and spiritual commitments she made. Anyone desiring to be successful can

Choices. Providence.

learn from Ruth's example of commitment.

Her allegiance to Naomi's family is demonstrated at three levels of commitment. First, she made a *physical commitment* to Naomi when she said: "*wherever you go, I will go; and wherever you lodge, I will lodge.*" Her second commitment was on a *social* level: "*your people shall be my people.*" Her final pledge was a *spiritual commitment*: "*your God, will be my God.*" To demonstrate the permanence of her commitment, Ruth said: "*Where you die, I will die, and there will I be buried. The LORD do so to me, and more also, if anything but death parts you and me.*"

There are a couple of lessons we can take away from the life of Ruth. Those three commitments allowed Ruth to remain faithful to her promise even when things in her life was falling apart. Her father-in-law died, her husband died, her mother-in-law decided to move to another country, and her sister-in-law turned her back on them. Inspite of those challenges Ruth remained faithful to her promises. She made a personal commitment to be with this family and will not disappoint Naomi.

Secondly, Ruth remained steadfast to her promise even when the future did not look too good. At one point Naomi expressed her grief about the difficulties their family was experiencing. Then she told Orpah and Ruth of how bleak the future looks and that they should just return home, get married, and start their lives over again. Orpah turned back to her people and her gods but Ruth stayed with Naomi.

Life is filled with choices. We are often challenge to make choices in the midst of life's difficulties. Take a page from the life of Ruth and discover how to face life's toughest challenges and succeed. An unwavering commitment to a set of values regardless of past difficulties, present trials, or the prospects of an uncertain future, will cause us to live triumphantly.

When we read the story of Ruth, its easy for us to walk away thinking 'that only happened to her because she's in the Bible.' We believe that such achievements will not come our way because we are not great people. Bu that is not true. Ruth was an ordinary person, just like Mother Teresa. It was their decision to remain faithful to their promises that set them apart.

The thing that keeps you and me from experiencing such success in our lives may be the simple fact of our willingness to remain faithful to the promises we have made. Whenever our circumstances get tough we move on, instead of 'staying the course' and remain faithful to our pledge.

Have you made an unconditional commitment in any area of your life? If not, you will continue to live the ordinary life constantly drifting in the circumstances of life.

Ruth made the big decision. She decided to put her trust in the Lord and remain faithful to her godly commitment while leaving the outcome in His hands.

Virtue. Blessing.

Unit 1, Chapter 1

Unit 1 • Lesson 1

let the *Scripture* speak, the discipline of biblical knowledge

Identify the Facts

1. Name three of the main characters in this story? _____

2. How long did Elimelech's family live in Moab? (1:1-5) _____

3. What happened to Elimelech in Moab? (1:1-5) _____

4. What happened to Mahlon in Moab? (1:1-5) _____

5. What happened to Chilion in Moab? (1:1-5) _____

6. Why did Naomi decide to return to the land of Judah? (1:6-10) _____

7. Elimelech and his family were from what city? (1:1-5) _____

8. What were the names of the sons of Elimelech and Naomi? (1:1-5) _____

9. What did Naomi, Orpah, and Ruth set out to do? (1:6-10) _____

10. On their way to the land of Judah, what did Naomi encourage her daughters-in-law to do? (1:6-10) _____

11. How did the ladies respond to Naomi? (1:6-10) _____

12. Why did Naomi encourage the ladies to return to Moab? (1:11-13)

Choices. Providence.

Making Good Decisions in Bad Times

13. How many times did Naomi encourage them to return to Moab? (1:11-13)

14. How many times did Orpah and Ruth cry? (include references) (1:11-15)

15. Why was Naomi grieving? (1:11-13) _____

16. (a) How did Orpah respond to Naomi's request to return to Moab? (b) How did Ruth respond to the same request? (1:14-18)

    (a) _____

    (b) _____

17. What was Naomi advice to Ruth concerning Orpah? (1:14-18)

18. What was Ruth's response to Naomi? (1:14-18) _____

19. Naomi and Ruth traveled until they arrived in the City of _____

20. How did the city receive the women? (1:14-18) _____

21. Naomi requested that the people of the City call her by what name? _____

22. What was Naomi's reason for her name change? (1:19 22)

23. Naomi: "I went out _____ the Lord brought me home _____

24. At what season did Naomi and Ruth return to Bethlehem? (1:19-22)

Virtue. Blessing.

Unit 1, Chapter 1

Unit 1 • Lesson 2

let the *Spirit* speak, the discipline of biblical interpretation

Draw Good Conclusions

1. Why did Elimelech move his family to Moab? Was it a bad decision? (1:1-5)

    (a) _____

    (b) _____

2. List 2 decisions that were made in the first five verses. (1:1-5)

    (a) _____

    (b) _____

3. Make a list of at least four major crises occurring in chapter 1.

    (a) _____

    (b) _____

    (c) _____

    (d) _____

4. What good fortunes occurred in this chapter? (1:1-22)

    _____

    _____

    _____

    _____

    _____

Choices. Providence.

Making Good Decisions in Bad Times

5. Why did Ruth decide to move to Bethlehem with Naomi? (1:6-18)

   _____

   _____

   _____

   _____

6. How did Naomi respond to Ruth's decision? (1:16-18) _____

   _____

7. How did the people greet Naomi? (19-22) _____

8. Describe Naomi's condition when she left and when she returned? (19-22)

   (a) _____   (b) _____

9. According to Naomi, how did the Lord treat her? (1:19-22) _____

   _____

10. When did Naomi and Ruth return to Bethlehem? (1:19-22) _____

    _____

Virtue. Blessing.

Unit 1, Chapter 1

Unit 1 • Lesson 3

let your Self speak, the discipline of biblical application

Apply Godly Principles

1. How should Elimelech have handled the famine in Judah? What other choices could he have made? (1:1-22)

2. Give a brief account of a time when you had to made a major decision for your family that was difficult but you trusted God instead of trying to work things out yourself (like Elimelech did).

Choices. Providence.

Making Good Decisions in Bad Times

3. Do Christians today make decisions the same way Elimelech did? If so, explain.

4. Give 2 examples of situations that require the kind of decision Ruth made in 1:16-18.

5. What do you learn about Ruth from the way she made her decision to travel to Bethlehem with Naomi and take up residence there?

Virtue. Blessing.

Unit 1, Chapter 1

Fill-In The Blank

1. In the days the _____ ruled in Bethlehem, Judah. (1:1-5)

2. Elimelech moved his family to the country of _____. (1:1-5)

3. Elimelech's wife was _____, and his two sons were _____ and _____. (1:1-5)

4. The family was from the city of _____. (1:1-5)

5. Naomi's sons were married to _____, and _____. (1:1-5)

6. Elimelech, Mahlon and Chilion _____ in Moab (1:1-5)

7. Orpah and Ruth said to Naomi, "Surely we will return with you to your _____." (1:6-10)

8. Orpah _____ her mother-in-law, but Ruth _____ to her. (1:14-18)

9. And she said, "Look, your sister-in-law has gone back to her _____ and to her _____." (1:14-18)

10. But Ruth said: (1:14-18) "_____ me not to _____ you, or to turn back from _____ after you; "for wherever you _____, I will _____; and wherever you _____, I will _____; your _____ shall be my _____, and your _____, my _____.

11. Naomi and Ruth traveled all the way to _____. (1:19-22)

12. When Naomi and Ruth arrived in Bethlehem, all the city was _____ because of them. (1:19-22)

13. Naomi said the Almighty has dealt very _____ with her. (1:19-22)

14. Naomi and Ruth went to _____ at the beginning of _____ harvest. (1:19-22)

Choices. Providence.

Making Good Decisions in Bad Times

MULTIPLE CHOICE

1. Naomi decided to return to Bethlehem, Judah because
   a. She heard that God had given them bread
   b. She was afraid to remain in Moab
   c. The Moabites asked her to leave the country
   d. None of the above

2. Orpah decided to return to Moab because
   a. Ruth told her to return home
   b. She was not well enough to travel
   c. She did not have any relatives in Bethlehem
   d. None of the above

3. These were the words of Ruth
   a. "Go, return each to her mother's house."
   b. "Entreat me not to leave you, or to turn back from following after you."
   c. "Bring the shawl that is on you and hold it."
   d. None of the above

4. Which of these gestures did Orpah give to Naomi before she returned to Moab?
   a. Waved goodbye
   b. Clung to her
   c. Kissed her
   d. None of the above

5. Which of these gestures best described Ruth's gesture to Naomi before they journeyed to Bethlehem?
   a. Waved goodbye
   b. Clung to her
   c. Kissed her
   d. None of the above

6. Which of these statements did Orpah made to Naomi?
   a. "Entreat me not to leave you, Or to turn back from following after you."
   b. "Your people shall be my people, and your God, my God."
   c. "I went out full, and the LORD has brought me home again empty."
   d. None of the above

Virtue. Blessing.

Unit 1, Chapter 1

MATCHING

Choose a word from the answers below *that best fits* on the blank line provided. Use each answer once. Answers to these items are all based on events in this chapter. Include one or more references with your answer.

1. _____ moved his family from Bethlehem to the land of Moab.
2. _____ a citizen of Moab.
3. _____ left Moab and returned to Bethlehem, Judah.
4. _____ Ephrathites of Bethlehem who married a Moabitess.
5. _____ arrived in Bethlehem with Naomi.
6. _____ happy about Naomi's return.
7. _____ a word that expressed the bitterness Naomi felt.
8. _____ Naomi and Ruth arrived at the beginning of this harvest.
9. _____ the rulers 'in those days'.

Answers: Mara, Ruth, Elimelech, Perez, Barley, City, Judges, Mahlon, Naomi, Orpah, Boaz

TRUE OR FALSE

Circle the best answer as True or False. If the answer is false, enter the correct answer on the blank line.

1. T F Elimelech decided to move his family back to Judah. _____
2. T F Naomi accompanied her husband to the land of Moab. _____
3. T F Naomi decided to leave her daughters-in-law and return to Judah. _____
4. T F Naomi pleaded with her daughters-in-law to return home. _____
5. T F Elimelech and his family were Moabites. _____
6. T F Ruth refused Naomi's invitation and returned to Moab. _____
7. T F The city was excited that Naomi returned to Bethlehem. _____
8. T F Elimelech's sons married Moabites. _____
9. T F Naomi and Ruth returned to Bethlehem during a severe famine. _____
10. T F Orpah decided to move to Judah with Naomi. _____

Choices. Providence.

Making Good Decisions in Bad Times

UNIT OVERVIEW

1. Where did most of the events in chapter 1 take place? (*Give specific locations.*)
   _____
   _____

2. When did the events in the book of Ruth take place? (1:1-5) _____
   _____
   _____

3. To whom was this book written? _____

4. Why was this book written? _____
   _____
   _____
   _____

5. Name four other books in the Bible that record the events found in Ruth?
   _____   _____
   _____   _____

6. Why did Ruth accompany Naomi to Bethlehem? _____
   _____
   _____
   _____

Virtue. Blessing.

Unit 1, Chapter 1

Talking Points

While you are going through your study of this Unit, use what you discover during your personal study and group discussions to write a sentence for each of the following. Use one or more of the following phrases to help with your discussion.

1. An Idea to explain. _____

2. A Principle I can apply. _____

3. A Story to be told. _____

4. A Goal to pursue. _____

5. A Job to complete. _____

6. An Outstanding individual. _____

7. An Example to follow. _____

Insights

Take a look at the whole chapter. Identify when the writer changes from one subject to another. Make a list of 1-3 subjects you find in this chapter.

1. Verses _____   Subject _____

2. Verses _____   Subject _____

3. Verses _____   Subject _____

Choices. Providence.

Making Good Decisions in Bad Times

Crossword Puzzle

CHAPTER 1

Answers to these questions are based on the *New King James* version.

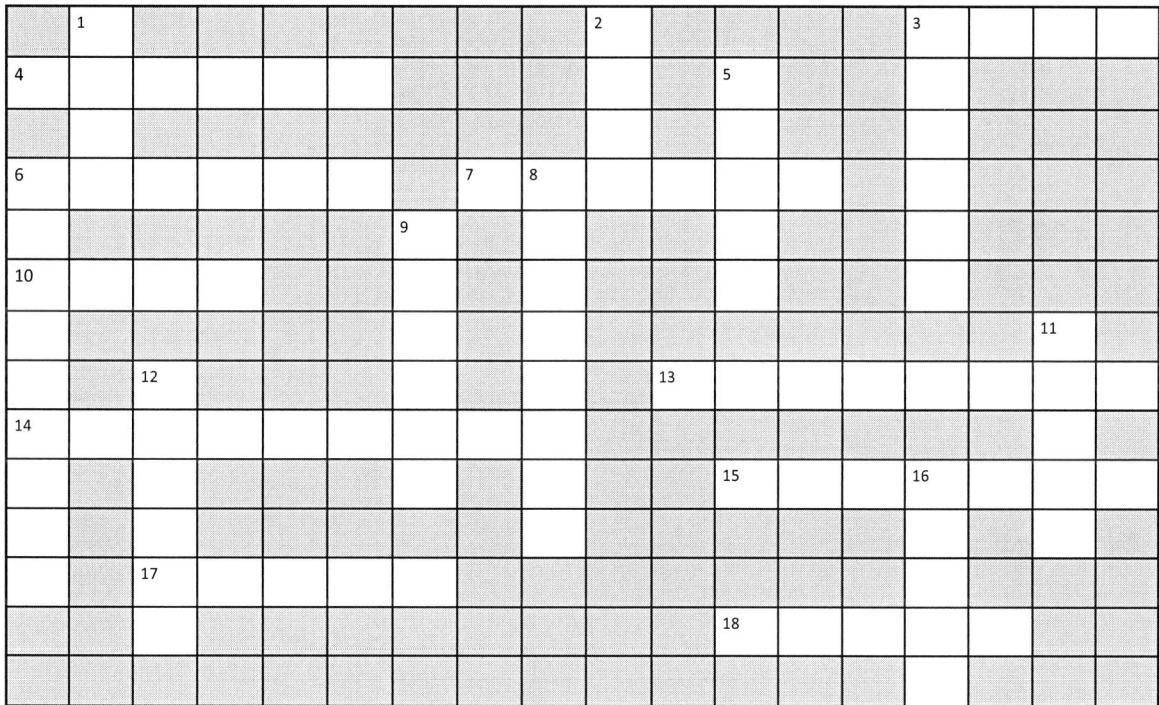

ACROSS

3. Naomi's condition when she left in Bethlehem
4. came upon the land of Bethlehem Judah when the Judges ruled
6. returned to Judah at the beginning of this harvest
7. Ruth's first husband
10. Naomi: "Go, _____" to your mother's house
13. Naomi's description of how the Lord dealt with her
14. relocated his family to the land of Moab
15. Elimelech's relationship to Naomi
17. Naomi's condition upon arrival in Bethlehem
18. Deserted Naomi and Ruth

DOWN

1. Naomi's name for herself
2. The daughter-in-law who stayed with Naomi
3. Elimelech's relationship to Mahlon and Chilion
5. Orpah and Ruth's mother-in-law
6. Hometown of Elimelech's family
8. Naomi's title for the Lord
9. the rulers of Judah
11. Ruth's gesture to Naomi just before they journeyed to Bethlehem
12. Orpah's gesture to Naomi before returning to Moab
16. God's gift to his people

Virtue. Blessing.

Unit 1, Chapter 1

WORD SEARCH PUZZLE
Chapter 1

J	U	D	G	E	S	S	D	D	N	O	I	L	I	H	C	A
E	D	H	E	L	I	M	E	L	E	C	H	C	L	U	N	G
B	E	G	I	N	N	I	N	G	Z	Y	T	P	M	E	H	F
X	K	D	E	M	U	C	D	N	A	B	S	U	H	B	Q	Y
Z	S	E	P	O	G	L	S	U	S	N	O	L	H	A	M	L
B	U	S	H	A	V	D	E	T	E	R	M	I	N	E	B	R
A	R	S	R	B	I	V	I	S	I	T	E	D	B	T	M	E
L	V	I	A	I	G	T	F	A	M	I	N	E	W	D	O	T
M	I	K	T	T	N	T	E	S	T	I	F	I	E	D	W	T
I	V	D	H	E	I	G	M	E	H	E	L	H	T	E	B	I
G	E	E	I	S	W	D	A	U	G	H	T	E	R	S	L	B
H	D	I	T	D	O	J	U	D	A	H	N	D	M	A	R	A
T	P	R	E	S	L	J	D	K	J	T	A	H	A	P	R	O
Y	A	U	S	F	L	U	I	C	R	E	T	P	E	W	E	I
S	X	B	N	A	O	M	I	E	R	C	O	U	N	T	R	Y
Y	D	O	Q	F	F	J	A	B	O	W	Y	E	L	R	A	B
U	I	C	I	D	E	T	C	I	L	F	F	A	H	T	U	R

Afflicted	determine	Mara	Almighty
Elimelech	Moabites	barley	empty
Naomi	beginning	entreat	Orpah
Bethlehem	Ephrathites	Ruth	bitterly
Famine	survived	bread	following
testified	buried	husband	visited
Chilion	Judah	wept	clung
Judges	womb	country	kissed
daughters	Mahlon		

Choices. Providence.

Unit 2, Chapter 2

Unit 2 • Lesson 1

let the Scripture speak, the discipline of biblical knowledge

Identify the Facts

1. What are three things we learn about Boaz in the first verse?

    (a) _____

    (b) _____

    (c) _____

2. What does Ruth ask Naomi's permission to do? (Verse 2)

    _____

3. What phrases do Boaz and the reapers use to greet each other? (Verse 4)

    Boaz: _____

    Reapers: _____

4. What does Boaz ask the servant who is in charge of the reapers? (Verse 5)

    _____

5. In verses 6-7, how does the servant describe Ruth?

    _____

6. What does Boaz ask Ruth to do in verses 8-9?

    _____

7. Why did Ruth think it was odd that Boaz would take notice of her? (Verse 10)

    _____

    _____

    _____

Virtue. Blessing.

Following the Hand of Providence

8. In verse 10, how did Ruth react to Boaz's instructions and requests?
   _____

9. What had Boaz heard about Ruth, according to verse 11?
   _____

10. Whom did Boaz say Ruth had sought for refuge in verse 12? _____

11. What did Boaz wish for Ruth in verse 12? _____

12. How does Ruth respond in verse 13? _____
    _____

13. What did Boaz provide at mealtime? (Verse 14) _____

14. What as Boaz's instructions to his workers in verses 15-16? _____
    _____

15. How much barley did Ruth glean? _____

16. What did Ruth do with what she had gleaned and the leftovers from her meal? (18)
    _____

17. What question and comment did Naomi make when she saw what Ruth had? (19)
    _____

18. What was Naomi's reaction to learning about Boaz's kindness? (Verse 20)
    _____

19. What are two or three things Ruth continued to do, according to verse 23?
    (a) _____
    (b) _____
    (c) _____

Choices. Providence.

Unit 2, Chapter 2

Unit 2 • Lesson 2

let the *Spirit* speak, the discipline of biblical interpretation

Draw Good Conclusions

1. Look at verse 13. What are some things you might be able to tell about Ruth prior to her conversation with Boaz? Did she think she was equal to a servant, or maybe a little lower in status? Could she have been worried about what would happen to her?

   _____
   _____
   _____

2. In verse 2, what do you think about Ruth asking for permission to go gather food among people she didn't know?

   _____
   _____

3. Why do you suppose the workers and Boaz mention the Lord in their greetings?

   _____

4. What are some things the servant in charge noticed about Ruth just from that day?

   _____

5. What was the purpose of Boaz's instructions to Ruth in verses 8-9?

   _____
   _____

6. Did Ruth take the instruction well? How would you describe her attitude in verse 10?

Virtue. Blessing.

Following the Hand of Providence

7. Verse 5 tells us Boaz didn't know Ruth by sight. But what does verse 11 say to you about one way he knew her? _____

8. Judging by verse 12, what did Boaz think of Ruth's reputation?

9. How would you describe Boaz's character, judging by verse 14-16?

10. What do verses 17-18 tell you about Ruth's character?

11. In Chapter 1, Naomi describes herself as bitter. Do you notice any possible changes in end of Chapter 2?

Choices. Providence.

Unit 2, Chapter 2

Unit 2 • Lesson 3

let your *Self* speak, the discipline of biblical application

Apply Godly Principles

1. Ruth didn't wait around for someone to take care of her and Naomi. What are some characteristics of Ruth we might need to put into practice in our lives?

   _____
   _____

2. Do you think how we greet one another is important? Would you be considered odd if you incorporated a blessing of some sort into your conversations with people?

   _____
   _____

3. In verse 6, the servant had noticed Ruth's work ethic on that day. In verse 11, Boaz tells what he had learned from others about Ruth. How important to you is your reputation? Is your reputation based only on things you did in the past, or also on things you might do today?

   _____
   _____

4. The servant said good things about Ruth and Boaz told Ruth about how impressed he was with her. Yet, Ruth reacts with humility. How do you take complements?

   _____
   _____

5. In verse 12, Boaz wishes good things for Ruth and in verse 14-16 he follows through to make sure his own wish for her, to some degree, is carried out. When you pray for people are you prepared to be the answer to those prayers? How can you be more active in hoping or pray-

Virtue. Blessing.

Following the Hand of Providence

er for the best?

_____

_____

6. What do you think Ruth's motives were for going out to work? Who did it benefit? Are there things you can do for church that benefit you and others? What are some of those things? How about things you can do at home, school or work which benefit neighbors, co-workers, friends or family?

_____

_____

7. What are one or two adjectives you would use to describe Ruth? Boaz? Are there any of these descriptions that don't describe you? What are some things we can do to be more like them?

_____

_____

8. How did Boaz's treatment of Ruth affect Naomi? _____

_____

_____

9. Why do you suppose Boaz just didn't hand grain to Ruth to take home instead of having her follow the servants and pick up grain? _____

_____

_____

Choices. Providence.

Unit 2, Chapter 2

FILL-IN THE BLANK

1. Boaz returned from Bethlehem, and said to the reapers, "The _____ be with _____." The Lord repay your work, and a full _____ be given you by the Lord God of Israel, under whose _____ you have come for _____.

2. Ruth said to Naomi, "The man's name with whom I worked today was _____

3. "Blessed be he of the Lord, who has not forsaken His _____ to the _____ and the _____."

4. Boaz was a relative of Naomi's _____

5. Boaz was a man of great _____

6. Ruth went to glean in the field of _____

7. Boaz arrived from the city of _____

8. Boaz asked his servant, "Whose _____ _____ is this?"

9. What meal did Boaz share with Ruth? _____

10. What time of day did Ruth finished her gleaning? _____

11. How much barley did she glean? _____

12. For how long was Ruth encouraged to glean? _____

13. Ruth was gleaning closely beside the young _____

14. Ruth lived at home with _____

Virtue. Blessing.

Following the Hand of Providence

MULTIPLE CHOICE

1. Boaz was a citizen of Judah. Which of the following phrases also describe Boaz?

    a. a man of great wealth

    b. a relative of Elimelech

    c. had several servants

    d. all of the above

    e. none of the above

2. Ruth requested to glean in the field of Boaz because

    a. she was invited by Boaz

    b. the servants called her to glean with them

    c. she hope to find favor with Boaz

    d. none of the above

3. Boaz arrived in his field from which city?

    a. Moab

    b. Bethlehem

    c. Tecumseh

    d. Nazareth

    e. none of the above

4. What was Boaz's question to the servant who was in charge of the field?

    a. "How many workers are in the field today?"

    b. "Is the harvest over?"

    c. "Whose young woman is this?"

    d. "Is Naomi gleaning with us today?"

    e. None of the above

5. Boaz said to Ruth

    a. do not go to glean in another field

    b. stay close by my young women

    c. follow behind the young women

    d. go to the vessels and drink from what the young men have drawn

    e. none of the above

    f. all of the above

Choices. Providence.

Unit 2, Chapter 2

6. Ruth fell on her face, bowed down to the ground. Which of these did she speak to Boaz?
    a. It has been fully reported to me, all that you have done for your mother-in-law.
    b. The LORD repay your work, and a full reward be given you by the LORD God of Israel
    c. Why have I found favor in your eyes?
    d. Where have you gleaned today?
    e. This man is a relation of ours, one of our close relatives.
    f. All of the above
    g. None of the above

7. Boaz told Ruth she has come to take refuge
    a. In his fields
    b. In the wealthy city of Bethlehem
    c. under the Lord's wings
    d. with Elimelech's family
    e. None of the above
    f. All of the above

8. Which of these statements are true of Ruth?
    a. she gleaned in the field until evening
    b. she beat out what she had gleaned
    c. she had about one ephah of barley
    d. she gave some barley to Naomi
    e. all of the above
    f. none of the above

9. Which of these items were on Boaz's dinner menu?
    a. bread, vinegar
    b. cake, ice cream
    c. chicken, chips
    d. none of the above
    e. all of the above

Virtue. Blessing.

Following the Hand of Providence

Matching

Choose a word from the **Answers** below that best fits on the blank line provided. Use each answer once. These sentences are taken from *chapter 2*. (include one or more references)

1. _____ time of day when reapers usually finished gleaning.

2. _____ a relative of Naomi's husband and a man of great wealth.

3. _____ "It is the young Moabite woman who came back with Naomi from the country of Moab."

4. _____ gleaning in the field of Boaz

5. _____ "Please let me go to the field, and glean heads of grain after him in whose sight I may find favor."

6. _____ "Go, my daughter."

7. _____ commanded not to touch Ruth

8. _____ Ruth reported to her on the day's events. (2:9)

9. _____ Ruth gathered after the reapers among these. (2:7)

10. _____ Boaz instructed Ruth to keep her eyes on this place. (2:9)

11. _____ one of Ruth's name for herself in chapter 2. (2:10)

Answers: mother-in-law, Boaz, Ruth, relative, Naomi, servant, morning, sheaves, Reapers, Elimelech, young men, field, evening, Mahlon, foreigner

Choices. Providence.

True or False

Circle the best answer as True or False. If the answer is false, enter the correct answer on the blank line.

1. T F Ruth just wanted to get out the house and away from Naomi. _____
2. T F Ruth just wanted to get out the house and away from Naomi. _____
3. T F The servant told Boaz what Ruth's name was. _____
4. T F The only person who called Ruth by name in Chapter 2 is Naomi. _____
5. T F Ruth wanted to be treated at least as an equal to Boaz's servants. _____
6. T F After running out of food, Ruth went to a different field to glean. _____
7. T F Boaz told his servants to hand bundles of grain to Ruth. _____
8. T F Boaz was a poor, unfamiliar citizen of Moab. _____
9. T F Naomi encouraged Ruth to glean in the filed of Boaz. _____
10. T F Boaz told his servants to keep Ruth away from his field. _____
11. T F Boaz told his Ruth that he knows nothing about her. _____
12. T F Ruth was hoping to find favor from Boaz. _____
13. T F Ruth was invited to have breakfast with Boaz. _____
14. T F Ruth gleaned in the field of Boaz until evening. _____
15. T F Naomi though Ruth should work only in Boaz's filed. _____

Virtue. Blessing.

Unit Overview

This section is provided for you to reflect on the things you have learned in your study of this chapter.

1. In your own words, describe what happens in Ruth 2. _____
   _____
   _____
   _____
   _____
   _____
   _____

2. How could you use this chapter to encourage a friend or family member about how people should treat each other?
   _____
   _____
   _____
   _____
   _____

3. What motivated Ruth to go out and work? For whom was she doing this?
   _____
   _____
   _____
   _____

Choices. Providence.

Unit 2, Chapter 2

4. Look at James 2:15-16. Compare that to Ruth 2:12 and 2:14-16. Is Boaz a good example of what James instructed Christians to be like? Why or why not?

5. What were some of the consequences of Boaz's kindness to Ruth in Chapter 2?

Virtue. Blessing.

Following the Hand of Providence

TALKING POINTS

While you are going through your study of this Unit, use what you discover during your personal study and group discussions to write a sentence for each of the following.

1. A *subject* I should discuss _____

2. A *command* I should obey _____

3. A *warning* I should heed _____

4. An *instruction* I should follow _____

5. A *Story* I should tell. _____

INSIGHTS

Take a look at the whole chapter. Identify when the writer changes from one subject to another. Make a list of 1-3 subjects you find in this chapter.

1. Verses _____ Subject _____
2. Verses _____ Subject _____
3. Verses _____ Subject _____

Choices. Providence.

Unit 2, Chapter 2

CROSSWORD PUZZLE

Answers to these questions are based on the *New King James* version.

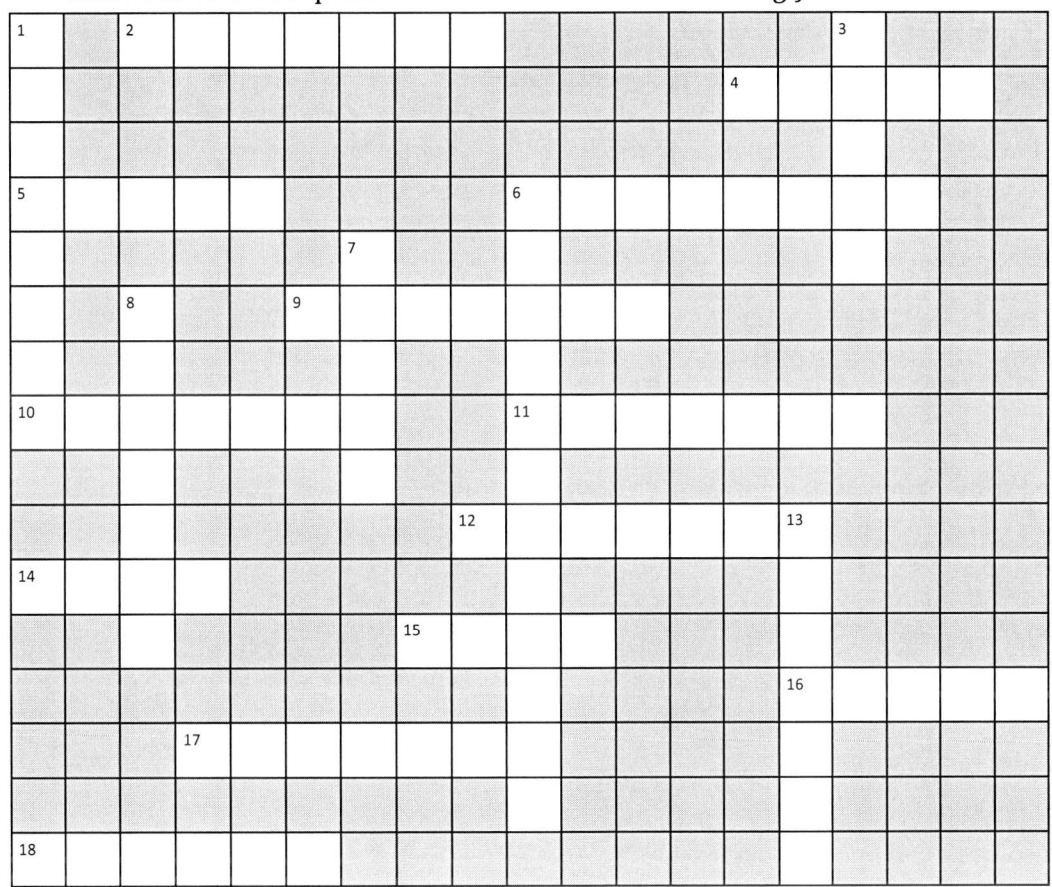

ACROSS

2. Gather the barley harvested in sets
4. Ruth lived with her after moving to Bethlehem
5. Ruth requested to glean heads of these
6. Nationality of Mahlon and Chilion's wives
9. the time Ruth started gleaning
10. Boaz spoke to his servant in charge of them
11. Ruth requested to glean among these
12. kind of food Boaz offered to Ruth at mealtime
14. The daughter-in-law who stayed with Naomi
15. A wealthy man in Bethlehem, relative of Elimelech's family
16. what Ruth requested to find in the sight of Boaz
17. The season when Naomi and Ruth arrived in Bethlehem
18. the manner in which Boaz spoke to Ruth

DOWN

1. Naomi's title for Ruth
3. Ruth's gesture in the presence of Boaz
6. Women working in the field
7. the place Ruth rested between gleaning
8. the nationality of the woman revealed to Boaz
13. sometime Ruth experienced from Boaz

Virtue. Blessing.

Following the Hand of Providence

WORD SEARCH PUZZLE

CHAPTER 2

F	L	O	X	B	Q	K	F	O	R	S	A	K	E	N	J	R	B	S	M
Q	H	S	E	R	V	A	N	T	I	G	L	E	A	N	Z	A	O	B	R
F	L	O	X	B	Q	K	F	O	R	S	A	K	E	N	J	R	B	S	M
Q	H	S	E	R	V	A	N	T	I	G	L	E	A	N	Z	A	O	B	R
Q	C	T	Z	L	V	K	J	Q	N	F	R	X	R	U	K	A	V	Q	D
P	O	H	E	Q	D	H	F	I	N	I	S	H	E	D	G	X	G	M	E
E	M	V	N	M	F	E	R	D	F	K	P	D	E	S	S	E	L	B	I
S	F	Y	G	F	I	C	D	R	E	L	A	T	I	V	E	S	J	E	F
G	O	L	N	K	E	T	R	N	C	K	M	G	G	U	W	D	N	Y	S
N	R	I	U	X	L	R	L	Q	A	B	R	N	R	R	R	V	Z	I	I
I	T	M	O	E	D	I	V	A	U	M	I	O	E	C	E	T	N	K	T
W	E	A	Y	S	P	C	V	N	E	N	M	W	W	Y	F	N	R	I	A
Z	D	F	B	R	K	H	D	E	E	M	A	O	L	S	U	A	Q	N	S
F	X	Y	K	X	E	L	A	V	S	R	T	E	C	E	G	V	G	D	I
Y	R	K	V	H	E	N	E	H	D	S	S	H	B	V	E	R	O	N	O
T	A	N	I	S	A	O	G	B	A	O	E	T	E	A	A	E	M	E	P
S	G	S	B	E	A	T	N	I	P	R	J	L	R	E	C	S	B	S	N
R	E	P	R	O	A	C	H	R	E	G	V	A	S	H	B	D	N	S	L
I	N	Y	A	P	E	R	U	B	M	R	W	E	T	S	M	I	I	F	X
H	I	F	U	R	S	P	A	G	O	F	O	W	S	E	J	A	A	D	P
T	V	B	B	N	E	T	S	I	L	E	Y	F	U	T	G	M	R	J	H
L	T	A	B	A	R	L	E	Y	U	I	S	R	A	E	L	G	G	R	F

barley	forsaken	reproach	beat
glean	reward	blessed	grain
Satisfied	Boaz	harvest	servant
bundles	Israel	sheaves	comforted
kindness	thirsty	commanded	listen
Vessels	ephah	maidservant	vinegar
evening	mealtime	wealth	family
purposely	wings	field	refuge
Worked	finished	relatives	young
foreigner	repay		

Choices. Providence.

Unit 3, Chapter 3

Unit 3 • Lesson 1

let the *Scripture* speak, the discipline of biblical knowledge

Identify the Facts

1. In verse 1, what does Naomi want for Ruth? _____

2. What instructions does Naomi give Ruth about her appearance? (3:3) _____

3. What instructions does Naomi give Ruth about when to show up? (3:3) _____

4. What did Naomi tell Ruth to do when Boaz lies down? (3:4) _____

5. Did Ruth agree to do what Naomi said? (verse 5) _____

6. Did Ruth do as she was told? (verse 6-7) _____

7. Did Naomi tell Ruth every detail that would happen that night? (verse 4) _____

8. When did Boaz wake up? (verse 8) _____

Virtue. Blessing.

Pursuing the Life of a Virtuous Woman

9. Did Boaz recognize Ruth right away? (verse 9) _____

10. What did Ruth say to Boaz? (verse 9) _____

11. How did Boaz respond to Ruth? (verse 10) _____

12. What did Boaz tell Ruth about her reputation? (verses 10-11) _____

13. What did Boaz explain to Ruth? (verses 12-13) _____

14. What did Boaz say to Ruth after she woke up and what did he do for her? (verses 14-15)

15. What was the reason Boaz gave Ruth the barley, according to verse 17?

16. What was Naomi's instruction to Ruth in verse 18? _____

Choices. Providence.

Unit 3, Chapter 3

Unit 3 • Lesson 2

let the *Spirit* speak, the discipline of biblical interpretation

Draw Good Conclusions

1. Is Naomi's attitude toward Ruth 3:1 different than in Ruth 1:6-13? _____

2. Do the instructions Naomi gives Ruth in the first four verses seem odd to you? Do you suppose they seemed strange to Ruth, who was from a different country?

3. What does Ruth want Boaz to do? _____

4. In Chapter 2, Boaz tells what others had told him about Ruth. What did he observe for himself? _____

5. What was the benefit of Ruth's reputation? _____

6. Did Boaz want to take care of Ruth? _____

7. What were proper steps Boaz needed to follow before he could take responsibility for Ruth?

Virtue. Blessing.

Pursuing the Life of a Virtuous Woman

8. How do you think Ruth and Boaz felt about each other at the point of Chapter 2? What are some things that might have happened if Boaz was not a man of good character?

9. Do you think Boaz reacted to Ruth with love, a sense of responsibility or both? Why?

10. Why do you think Boaz said in verse 14 that Ruth should not let it be known that she had been there, even though Naomi told her to go?

11. Why give Ruth more food if Boaz was not yet responsible for her well-being?

12. What does Naomi's statement about Boaz in verse 18 say about what Naomi thinks of Boaz?

Choices. Providence.

Unit 3, Chapter 3

Unit 3 • Lesson 3

let your *Self* speak, the discipline of biblical application

Apply Godly Principles

1. Naomi wanted what was best for Ruth and at the end of the chapter, Naomi also gets a blessing in the form of food. What does this tell us about looking out for others?

   _____
   _____
   _____

2. Ruth was obedient to Naomi's instructions, even though they may have seemed awkward and no result was guaranteed. What does that say about Ruth? How might Ruth's actions here be similar or different than your obedience to God? _____

   _____
   _____
   _____

3. What do you think Boaz liked most about Ruth? _____

   _____

4. What do Boaz's words and actions say about how he felt about Ruth? Can the people you love tell we love them just by our actions? What are some things you can do at church today that say "I love you" without using words? _____

   _____

Virtue. Blessing.

Pursuing the Life of a Virtuous Woman

5. Knowing his feelings about Ruth, why should Boaz care about what people thought about her being on the threshing floor? What are some things you can do to protect your relationships from being judged or whispered about? _____
_____

6. Ruth, nor Naomi were yet Boaz's responsibility, but he continued to provide for them both. What does his example tell us good people do for others? Is there someone you know of that you have the resources or time to help? _____
_____
_____
_____

Choices. Providence.

Unit 3, Chapter 3

Fill-In The Blank

1. "All that you _____ to me I _____ _____."

2. I will do all that you request, for all the people of my town know that you are a _____ _____.

3. For he said to me, do not go to _____ - _____ to your mother-in-law.

4. Naomi asked Ruth, "shall I not seek _____ for you, that it may be _____ with you?"

5. Boaz will be _____ barley that evening at the _____ floor.

6. Ruth was told to wash and anoint herself and to put on her best _____ and go to the _____ floor. (3:3)

7. Ruth was to conceal her identity until Boaz was finished _____ and _____.

8. After Boaz ate and drank, his _____ was _____.

9. After Boaz laid sown to sleep, Ruth came _____ beside him, _____ his feet, and lay down.

10. When Boaz awaken and realize she was beside him, he said "_____ _____ _____?"

11. Ruth said to Boaz, "I am _____, your _____. Take your _____ under your _____, for you are a close relative."

12. Boaz said to Ruth, "and now, my _____, do not _____. I will do for you all that you _____, for all the people of my town know that you are a _____ _____.

13. If the closer relative was willing to perform the _____ the next morning, that would be _____.

14. Boaz gave Ruth six _____ of _____ which she put in the _____ she had on her.

15. Ruth, "he said to me, 'Do not go _____-_____ to your _____.

16. "Sit still, my daughter, until you know how the matter will turn out; for the man will not _____ until he has concluded the matter _____ _____."

Virtue. Blessing.

Pursuing the Life of a Virtuous Woman

MULTIPLE CHOICE

1. Who said, "My daughter, shall I not seek security for you, that it may be well with you?"
   a. Elimelech
   b. Boaz
   c. Naomi
   d. None of the above

2. He was winnowing barley that tonight at the threshing floor.
   a. the Relative
   b. Boaz
   c. Chilion
   d. None of the above

3. Who spoke these words? "All that you say to me I will do."
   a. Ruth
   b. Naomi
   c. Orpah
   d. None of the above

4. Now it happened at midnight that the man was startled.
   a. the Relative
   b. Boaz
   c. Elimelech
   d. None of the above

5. Name the person who asked the following question. "Who are you?"
   a. Naomi
   b. Ruth
   c. Orpah
   d. None of the above

6. Who said this? "Take your maidservant under your wing, for you are a close relative."
   a. Naomi
   b. Boaz
   c. the Relative
   d. None of the above

7. Who spoke these words? "And now, my daughter, do not fear. I will do for you all that you request, for all the people of my town know that you are a virtuous woman."
   a. Naomi
   b. Ruth

Choices. Providence.

Unit 3, Chapter 3

       c. Boaz
       d. None of the above

8. "Do not let it be known that the woman came to the threshing floor."
    a. Servant of Boaz
    b. Naomi
    c. Ruth
    d. None of the above

9. Boaz requested that Ruth provide a container for the barley he was about to give her. Which of these container did she bring?
    a. burlap bag
    b. plastic bag
    c. shawl
    d. None of the above

10. Boaz's heart became merry after he had done which of the following?
    a. working the evening shift
    b. investing in a new business venture
    c. eating and drinking
    d. All of the above
    e. None of the above

11. Which of these statements best describes what the town people thought about Ruth?
    a. a relative of Elimelech's family
    b. a virtuous woman
    c. a worker in his field
    d. All of the above
    e. None of the above

12. Which of these statements did Boaz make to Ruth?
    a. "Who are you?"
    b. "Blessed are you of the LORD, my daughter!"
    c. "Bring the shawl that is on you and hold it."
    d. All of the above
    e. None of the above

13. Which of these statements did Naomi make to Ruth?
    a. "All that you say to me I will do."
    b. "Who are you?"
    c. "Bring the shawl that is on you and hold it."
    d. All of the above
    e. None of the above

Virtue. Blessing.

Pursuing the Life of a Virtuous Woman

Matching

Choose a word from the answers below *that best fits* on the blank line provided. Use each answer once. Answers to these items are all based on events in this chapter. Include one or more references with your answer. A word may be used more than once.

From 6-11, match the quote with the person who said it.

1. _____ what was Naomi seeking for Ruth?
2. _____ what was Boaz winnowing (inspecting) at the threshing floor?
3. _____ what was Ruth told to do to Boaz's feet?
4. _____ Ruth remained at the threshing floor until what time?
5. _____ Boaz's gift to Ruth's mother-in-law?
6. _____ "Shall I not seek security for you, that it may be well with you?
7. _____ "Blessed are you of the LORD, my daughter!"
8. _____ "Is that you, my daughter?"
9. _____ "All that you say to me I will do."
10. _____ "Take your maidservant under your wing, for you are a close relative."
11. _____ "Who are you?"
12. _____ Naomi wanted Ruth to wear one of her best.
13. _____ Ruth was to conceal her identity for a time from him.
14. _____ a phrase describing Naomi's relationship to Ruth.
15. _____ What was Ruth doing at the feet of Boaz?

Answers: garment, morning, lying, Barley, Naomi, barley, Chilion, security, Mahlon, Boaz, Mother-in-law, Ruth

Choices. Providence.

Unit 3, Chapter 3

True or False

Circle the best answer as True or False. If the answer is false, enter the correct answer on the blank line.

1. T   F   Naomi wanted Ruth to have security and well-being.   _____
2. T   F   Ruth improvised a little on what Naomi had instructed her to do.   _____
3. T   F   Boaz invited Ruth to lie down next to him.   _____
4. T   F   Ruth got up early, before anyone could recognize her.   _____
5. T   F   Boaz planned to go behind his relative's back to get Ruth.   _____
6. T   F   Ruth enjoyed a nice dinner with Boaz before Boaz went to sleep.   _____
7. T   F   Boaz promised to take responsibility of Ruth if his relative did not.   _____
8. T   F   Ruth requested to glean in the field of Elimelech's family.   _____
9. T   F   Naomi advised Ruth to stay away from this relative's field.   _____
10. T   F   Ruth happened to come to the field belonging to the relative.   _____
11. T   F   The name of the relative of Elimelech's family was Bozo.   _____
12. T   F   The servant said to Boaz: "Whose young woman is this?"   _____
13. T   F   Boaz went to the field but never took notice of Ruth.   _____
14. T   F   Boaz told Ruth to continue gleaning in his field.   _____
15. T   F   Naomi though Boaz was a stranger from the land of Oz.   _____
16. T   F   Naomi told Ruth it was a bad idea to go back to the field of Boaz.   _____
17. T   F   Ruth refused to return to glean in the field of Boaz.   _____

Virtue. Blessing.

Pursuing the Life of a Virtuous Woman

Unit Overview

1. Describe in your own words what happened in Chapter 3. _____
   _____
   _____
   _____

2. What are some of the over-riding themes of Chapter 3? _____
   _____
   _____
   _____

3. What was Ruth hoping Boaz would do? _____
   _____

4. What did Boaz say he would do? _____
   _____

5. What are a few things Boaz was concerned about as Ruth was leaving?
   _____
   _____
   _____

6. What was the process Boaz needed to go through before he could take full responsibility for Ruth? _____

7. What did Boaz promise to do? _____
   _____

8. By the end of Chapter 3, did Naomi feel good about Ruth's future? _____
   _____

Choices. Providence.

Unit 3, Chapter 3

TALKING POINTS

While you are going through your study of this Unit, use what you discover during your personal study and group discussions to write a sentence for each of the following. Use one or more of the following phrases to help with your discussion.

1. An Idea to explain. _____

2. A Principle I can apply. _____

3. A Story to be told. _____

4. A Goal to pursue. _____

5. A Job to complete. _____

INSIGHTS

Take a look at the whole chapter. Identify when the writer changes from one subject to another. Make a list of 1-3 subjects you find in this chapter.

1. Verses _____   Subject _____

2. Verses _____   Subject _____

3. Verses _____   Subject _____

Virtue. Blessing.

Pursuing the Life of a Virtuous Woman

CROSSWORD PUZZLE
CHAPTER 3

Answers to these questions are based on the *New King James* version.

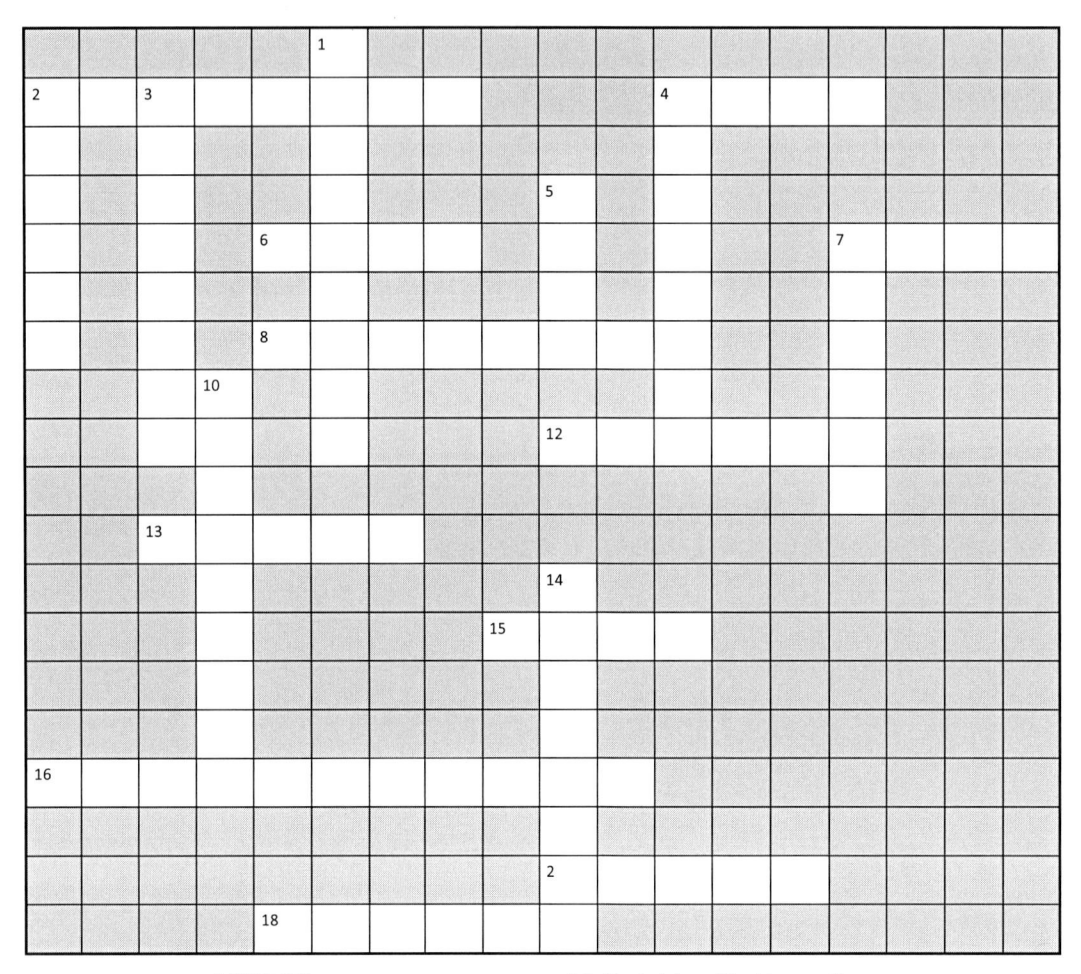

ACROSS
2. Naomi's desire for Ruth
4. Boaz and the Relative must fulfill their _____
6. Naomi wanted Ruth to meet him at the threshing floor
7. what Boaz and his servants did to the barley at the threshing floor
8. time Boaz was awaken from his sleep
12. quality of character the people saw in Ruth
13. what Boaz discovered at his feet
15. Ruth's destination after leaving the threshing floor
16. Ruth identified herself as one
17. Ruth brought this item to Boaz
18. Measurement of barley given to Ruth

DOWN
1. Boaz task at the threshing floor
2. the way Ruth approached Boaz's feet
3. Boaz's attitude after his dinner
4. Boaz's title for Ruth
5. Ruth wanted to be under Boaz's _____
7. Boaz's gift to Ruth
10. what Ruth did to the feet of Boaz
14. what quality of character was Ruth showing

Choices. Providence.

Unit 3, Chapter 3

Word Search Puzzle

Chapter 3

H	S	N	I	T	U	N	R	E	L	A	T	I	V	E	G	R	M
I	F	I	N	I	S	H	E	D	N	D	W	T	M	Q	N	D	I
M	R	A	N	R	Z	G	F	E	G	I	N	Y	R	M	I	E	D
S	E	N	S	S	C	S	T	A	N	A	B	Y	O	Y	D	R	N
E	V	S	H	G	M	A	R	N	V	M	O	E	F	F	R	U	I
L	O	W	A	J	E	M	O	R	A	G	A	R	R	U	O	S	G
F	C	E	W	U	E	W	E	T	T	X	N	E	E	Q	C	A	H
S	N	R	L	N	I	S	T	V	S	I	O	C	P	V	C	E	T
C	U	E	T	N	D	E	L	I	M	N	I	O	G	I	A	M	N
J	H	D	G	I	R	R	G	Y	G	S	N	G	N	R	T	D	V
S	D	E	A	X	K	O	N	T	N	T	T	N	I	T	H	H	K
R	T	M	E	G	C	O	I	I	I	R	E	I	N	U	A	A	I
A	E	A	I	R	P	L	W	R	H	U	P	Z	R	O	P	N	N
B	I	Q	R	H	F	F	A	U	S	C	A	E	O	U	P	D	D
B	Z	D	U	T	E	U	G	C	E	T	E	E	M	S	E	E	N
C	J	V	U	E	L	A	L	E	R	E	H	U	I	L	N	D	E
C	G	E	E	T	S	E	R	S	H	D	B	A	R	L	E	Y	S
N	A	M	O	W	Y	T	D	T	T	K	H	F	H	G	D	B	S

according	heap	relative	anoint
heart	request	answered	himself
Security	barley	instructed	shawl
cheerful	kindness	startled	duty
maidservant	threshing	eaten	matter
uncover	finished	measured	virtuous
floor	midnight	wing	garment
morning	winnowing	handed	perform
Woman	happened	recognize	

Virtue. Blessing.

Pursuing the Life of a Virtuous Woman

Unit 4 • Lesson 1

let the *Scripture* speak, the discipline of biblical knowledge

Identify the Facts

1. Where did the close Relative meet Boaz? (4:1-4) _____

2. What was Boaz doing when they met at the gate? (4:1-4) _____

3. How many men of the city did Boaz asked to sit with them. (4:1-4) _____

4. Who were these men? (What was their title?) (4:1-4) _____

5. What did Naomi sell? (4:1-4) _____

6. Who was owner of the item Naomi sold? (4:1-4) _____

7. If the Relative bought the land, what other transaction would he be required to fulfill? (4:5-12)
   _____

8. Why must the close Relative make the second transaction? (4:5-12) _____
   _____

9. What was the Relative's response to the proposal from Boaz? (4:5-12) _____

10. What was the Relative's reason for refusing Boaz's proposal? (4:5-12) _____
    _____

11. What was the Relative's advice to Boaz? (4:5-12) _____

12. What was the custom in Israel to confirm a transaction when a person would exchange or redeem something? (4:5-12) _____
    _____

13. In this case, who gave up the sandals? (Boaz or Relative (4:5-12) _____

14. According to verses 9-10, what transactions did Boaz make on that day?
    _____

Choices. Providence.

Unit 3, Chapter 3

15. From whom did Boaz purchased the land? (4:5-12) _____

16. The people and elders said they were _____ to this transaction. (4:5-12)

17. They hoped that Ruth would be like which two women in the Old Testament? (4:5-12)
_____ and _____

18. For what reason were these two women remembered? (4:5-12) _____
_____

19. They also wished/prayed Ruth would _____ in _____
and be _____ in Bethlehem. (4:5-12)

20. They prayed that Naomi's house would be like that of _____ the son of
_____ and _____ (4:5-12)

21. To Boaz and Ruth was born a _____

22. The women told Naomi that the Lord did not leave her without a close _____

23. The women prayed that the son would be _____ in Israel. (4:13-22

24. They prayed that he would be to Naomi a _____ of _____
and a _____ of her old age. (4:13-22)

25. What did Naomi do with the child? (4:13-21) _____

26. The women said *there was a child born to* _____ (4:13-21)

27. The women named the child _____ (4:13-21)

28. Obed was the father of _____ and grand-father of _____ (4:13-21)

29. List the genealogy of Boaz from Perez to David. (4:13-22)
(a) _____ (b) _____
(c) _____ (d) _____
(e) _____ (f) _____
(g) _____ (h) _____
(i) _____ (j) _____

30. Who said these words: "I will redeem it." (4:5-12) _____

31. Who said these words: "I cannot redeem it." (5-12) _____

Virtue. Blessing.

Unit 4, Chapter 4

Unit 4 • Lesson 2

let the *Spirit* speak, the discipline of biblical interpretation

Draw Good Conclusions

1. Why did Boaz invite the Relative and elders to the gate? (4:1-5) _____
   _____
   _____

2. What do you understand by the statement of Boaz in 4:5? _____
   _____
   _____
   _____
   _____

3. Why is the genealogy of Perez given in this book? (4:13-22) _____
   _____

4. Did the Relative make the right decision? (4:1-12) (Give reasons for your answer.)
   _____
   _____
   _____
   _____
   _____
   _____

Choices. Providence.

Accepting God's Blessings

5. Why did Boaz decide to redeem the property? (4:1-12) _____

6. What are some things you learn about Boaz from this chapter? (4:1-22)

    (a) _____

    (b) _____

    (c) _____

    (d) _____

7. What were the people's hope for Boaz? (4:11-22) _____

8. What were the women's final remarks about Naomi? (4:11-22)

9. How did Naomi respond to the birth of Obed? (4:13-22) _____

Virtue. Blessing.

Unit 4, Chapter 4

10. Choose two persons from this chapter (a male and female) and name one thing they did that is admirable.

    (a) _____

    _____

    (b) _____

    _____

11. How is Naomi's response to the events in chapter 4 different to her response of the events in chapter 1?

    _____

    _____

    _____

    _____

    _____

12. Chapter 4 records the beginning of several new experiences. Identify at least two of those experiences. _____

    _____

    _____

    _____

    _____

Choices. Providence.

Accepting God's Blessings

Unit 4 • Lesson 3

let your Self speak, the discipline of biblical application

Apply Godly Principles

1. What lessons have you learned from the persons listed below? How will you practice them?

   Boaz. _____

   _____

   _____

   Naomi. _____

   _____

   _____

   _____

   The People. _____

   _____

   _____

   The Women. _____

   _____

   _____

   Ruth. _____

   _____

   _____

   _____

2. Boaz was committed to the heritage of his family and willingly takes on the responsibility of

Virtue. Blessing.

Unit 4, Chapter 4

redeeming the property of Elimelech. As you look at your family, list two things you are doing (can do) to build a lasting legacy for your family. (Discuss the way Boaz went about fulfilling his responsibility. How will you arranged to fulfill your responsibility?)

a. _____

b. _____

3. List 3 common ways people abandon their families **and** 3 things you can do to strengthen your family.

Ways individuals abandon/weaken their families.

a. _____

b. _____

c. _____

Ways you can strengthen your family.

a. _____

b. _____

c. _____

Choices. Providence.

Accepting God's Blessings

Fill-In The Blank

1. Now Boaz went up to the _____ and sat down there.

2. Boaz invited the close _____ to sit with him at the gate.

3. Boaz took ten men of the _____ of the city, and said, "Sit down here."

4. Buy back the piece of land "in the presence of the _____ and the _____ of my people."

5. If you will redeem it, _____ it; but if you will not _____ it, then tell me, for there is no one but you to redeem it, and I am next after you."

6. And he said, "I will _____ it."

7. "I cannot _____ it for myself, lest I _____ my own _____."

8. In Israel, it was custom that a man confirm redeeming and exchanging by giving away his _____.

9. The elders of the city were _____ to the transaction between Boaz and the _____.

10. When Boaz redeemed the property, he obtained the right to marry _____.

11. Boaz redeemed the property to _____ the name of the family.

12. The Elders hoped that Ruth would become like _____ and _____.

13. The Elders hoped that Boaz may you _____ in Ephrathah and be _____ in Bethlehem.

14. After Boaz and Ruth were married, the LORD gave her _____, and she bore a _____.

15. The Lord gave Naomi a close _____.

16. Naomi took the child and laid him on her _____, and became a _____ to him.

17. The women said "There is a son born to _____." And they called his name _____. The "son" was the father of _____, and grand-father of _____.

Virtue. Blessing.

Unit 4, Chapter 4

MULTIPLE CHOICE

1. Boaz qualified to redeem the property from Elimelech's family because
   a. he was a close relative
   b. he had financial means
   c. he wanted to prolong the family heritage
   d. the person most qualified declined
   e. all of the above
   f. none of the above

2. One of the most important persons in chapter 4
   a. Elimelech
   b. Orpah
   c. Boaz
   d. Chilion
   e. None of the above

3. Sat at the gate with Boaz
   a. Relative
   b. David
   c. Obed
   d. Chilion
   e. None of the above

4. Sold the property to Boaz
   a. Ruth
   b. Elimelech
   c. Mahlon
   d. Naomi
   e. Orpah
   f. All of the above

5. An item given to confirm a redemption or exchanging between two parties
   a. Ring
   b. Sandal
   c. Cash
   d. Barley
   e. None of the above

6. The one who purchases the property from Naomi had was also obligated to
   a. Provide Naomi a job
   b. Marry Naomi
   c. Marry Ruth
   d. Move back to Moab
   e. None of the above

7. The close relative declined his right to
   a. Redeem the property
   b. Provide Ruth with a job
   c. Move Naomi back to Moab
   d. Marry Naomi
   e. None of the above

Choices. Providence.

Accepting God's Blessings

MATCHING

Choose a word from the answers below <u>that best fits</u> on the blank line provided. Use each answer once. Answers to these items are all based on events in chapter 4. Include one or more references with your answer.

1. _____ redeemed the rights to Elimelech's property and to marry Ruth.
2. _____ declined the responsibility to redeem the property of Elimelech.
3. _____ "a restorer of life and a nourisher of your old age."
4. _____ held the young child in her arm and became his nurse.
5. _____ widow of Mahlon and the wife of Boaz.
6. _____ witnesses to the transaction between Boaz and the relative.
7. _____ they said, "may his name be famous in Israel."

<u>Answers:</u> Naomi, Elders, City, Orpah, Mahlon, Boaz, Women, Judges, Obed, Ruth

TRUE OR FALSE

1. T F Boaz invited the Relative to sit with him at the gate. _____
2. T F Twelve elders sat at the gate with Boaz and the Relative. _____
3. T F At first, the relative did not want to redeem the property. _____
4. T F In confirming a transaction, one man gives his ring to the other. _____
5. T F Naomi sold all their property to Boaz. _____
6. T F According to chapter 4, Ruth was the widow of Chilion. _____
7. T F Naomi rejected the baby that was born to Boaz and Ruth. _____
8. T F Boaz redeemed the property to carry on the family's heritage. _____
9. T F The people of Bethlehem were happy about Ruth. _____
10. T F Boaz was the grand-father of David. _____
11. T F Jesse was the father of Obed. _____
12. T F The Relative was unwilling to marry Ruth. _____
13. T F Whoever bought Elimelech's field was supposed to marry Ruth. _____

Virtue. Blessing.

Unit 4, Chapter 4

Unit Overview

1. Who is the most influential person in this chapter? Why? (4:1-22)

   _____
   _____
   _____
   _____

2. What was the people's opinion about Ruth? (4:1-22) _____

   _____
   _____
   _____
   _____
   _____

3. List four significant events that take place in chapter 4.

   a. _____
   _____

   b. _____
   _____

   c. _____
   _____

   d. _____
   _____

Choices. Providence.

Accepting God's Blessings

4. The book of Ruth was most likely written about whom, and why? (4:13-22)

5. Discuss how Boaz's decision to redeem the property affected Elimelech's family heritage.

6. Why does the passage elaborates on the transaction between Boaz and the Relative but gives little details about the marriage of Boaz and Ruth?

Virtue. Blessing.

Unit 4, Chapter 4

Talking Points

While you are going through your study of this Unit, use what you discover during your personal study and group discussions to write a sentence for each of the following. Use one or more of the following phrases to help with your discussion.

1. An Idea to explain. _____
   _____

2. A Story to be told. _____
   _____
   _____

3. A Job to complete. _____
   _____

4. An important decision. _____
   _____
   _____

5. Outstanding individuals. _____ _____
   _____ _____

Insights

Take a look at the whole chapter. See if you can identify when the writer changes from one subject to another. Make a list of 1-3 subjects you find in this chapter.

1. Verses _____ Subject _____

2. Verses _____ Subject _____

3. Verses _____ Subject _____

Choices. Providence.

Accepting God's Blessings

Crossword Puzzle

CHAPTER 4

Answers to these questions are based on the *New King James* version.

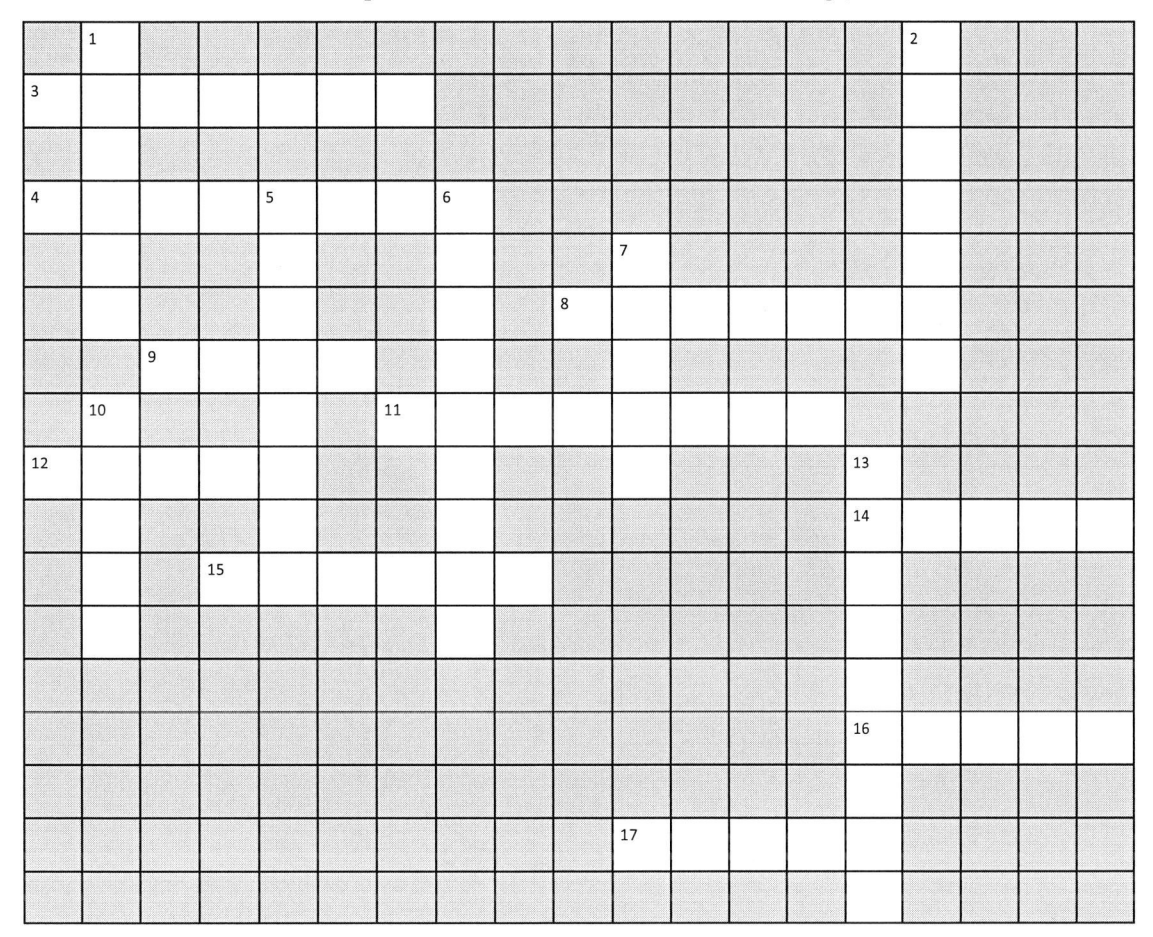

ACROSS

3. Given to confirm a transaction
4. They were witnesses to the transaction
8. Ruth's nationality
9. Went to the gate of the city and sat down
11. The women hope the child will be a ____ of life
12. Boaz purchased the field from her
14. Available for sale to a relative
15. The responsibility of the Relative or Boaz
16. Considered to be like Rachael and Leah
17. They spoke many word to Naomi

DOWN

1. Ruth was his widow
2. Built the house of Israel
5. He said: "I cannot redeem it."
6. Their job at the gate
7. Naomi's resting place for the child
10. The grandson of Obed
13. God's gift to Boaz and Ruth

Virtue. Blessing.

Word Search Puzzle

Chapter 4

B	O	S	O	M	N	O	I	T	I	S	O	P	L	D	C	C	A
B	R	O	T	H	E	R	R	E	L	A	T	I	V	E	C	Z	C
M	N	N	U	E	H	G	N	I	G	N	A	H	C	X	E	E	Q
N	O	O	B	E	L	O	N	G	E	D	N	W	O	D	I	W	U
O	R	T	I	V	O	S	E	S	S	E	N	T	I	W	F	P	I
I	E	O	S	T	V	D	O	L	R	G	S	E	N	O	E	I	R
T	H	F	Q	U	A	B	I	H	H	T	Q	U	L	R	Y	R	E
P	S	F	F	M	C	M	T	N	N	T	R	G	P	P	L	U	D
E	I	S	S	I	E	E	R	A	H	S	Z	E	R	T	O	J	L
C	R	P	C	A	R	E	T	I	E	E	T	K	E	Y	T	E	H
N	U	R	R	B	N	I	D	G	F	U	R	N	R	G	O	L	P
O	O	I	Z	O	B	D	N	E	A	N	E	I	O	O	G	P	P
C	N	N	L	A	B	U	A	T	R	V	O	M	T	L	E	O	R
H	L	G	H	F	O	H	E	L	E	B	I	C	S	A	B	E	O
I	X	N	I	Y	S	Z	G	S	P	F	V	B	E	E	N	P	S
L	I	S	P	O	K	E	N	I	H	Q	C	U	R	N	U	C	P
D	B	O	R	N	P	R	E	S	E	N	C	E	L	E	G	Z	E
M	U	T	H	G	U	O	B	U	N	N	H	T	Q	G	B	P	R

acquired	exchanging	presence	begot
genealogy	prosper	belonged	inhabitants
redeem	born	inheritance	relative
bosom	neighbor	restorer	bought
nourisher	sandal	brethren	nurse
seven	brother	offspring	spoken
child	people	widow	conception
people	witnesses	confirmation	perpetuate
young	custom	position	

Choices. Providence.

Exploring Ruth:

Finding hope, restoring Heritage presents a thirteen-week study of an Old Testament book that shows how God's grace can change your most difficult circumstances into something wonderful.

Author David Henry draws from more than twenty-five years of Bible teaching experience to craft a set of studies that explore how God gives hope to those who are obedient to Him through His word.

Thirteen weekly Bible studies are grouped into four units. Each unit begins by providing a focal passage, stating a big idea, suggesting key verses, offering a memory verse, and stating unit goals. Each unit moves from finding the facts to drawing good conclusions to applying biblical principles. Within each unit, the individual studies provide a variety of styles of questions, such as fill-in-the-blanks, multiple-choice, true-or-false, and wordsearch puzzles.

This study also seeks to help you develop your skills in studying the Bible. It is a good match for Christian education classes, small groups, midweek Bible studies, ministries in prisons and other mission fields, family devotions, and personal study. No matter what setting reflects your circumstances, you will discover God's grace revealed in Jesus Christ.

This guide presents an exploration of Ruth, leading the student to see how God guides, protects, and provides for those who are obedient to Him.

David Henry

earned a master's degree in advanced biblical studies from Southeastern Baptist Theological Seminary, Wake Forest, North Carolina. Over the last twenty-five years, he has served as a Bible teacher in Antigua, North Carolina, and Oklahoma. He lives in Shawnee, Oklahoma, with his wife, three daughters, and two grandchildren.

Virt